P9-EKY-796

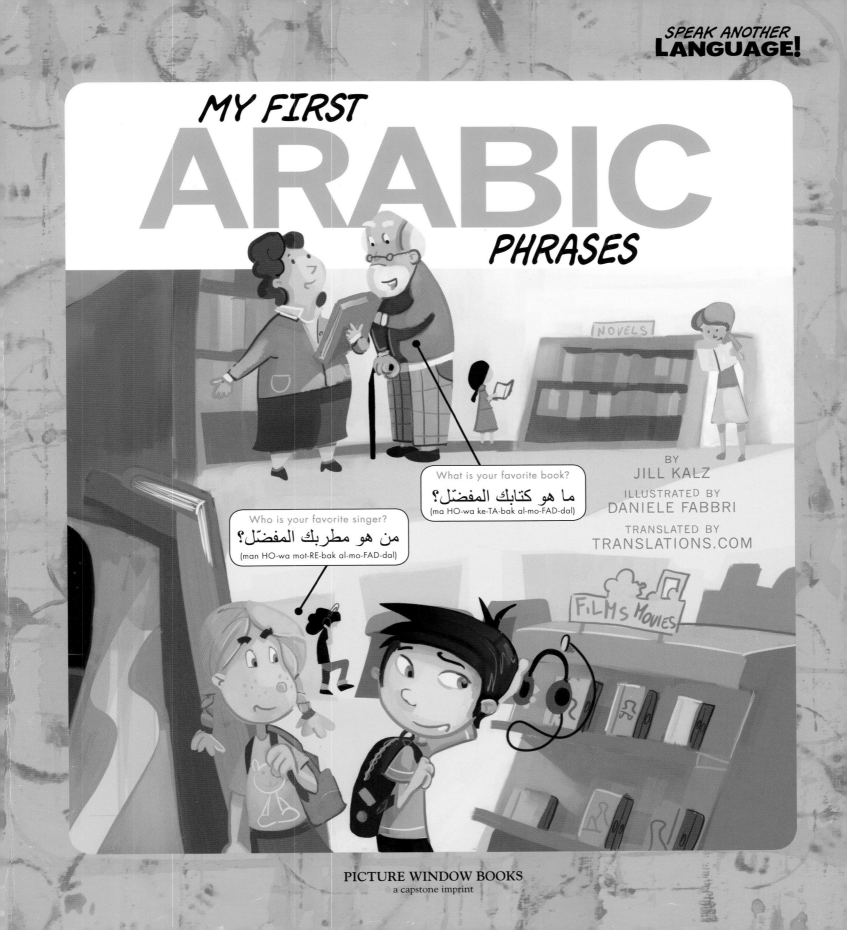

# TABLE OF CONTENTS

# HOW TO USE THIS DICTIONARY

This book is full of useful phrases in both English and Arabic. The English phrase appears first, followed by the Arabic phrase. Look below each Arabic phrase for help to sound it out. Try reading the phrases aloud.

Topic heading in English

Topic heading in Arabic

Additional phrases to learn

Phrase in English
**Phrase in Arabic**
(pronunciation)

## NOTES ABOUT THE ARABIC LANGUAGE

Arabic is written from right to left—the opposite of English. The Arabic writing system is cursive, so most letters are connected to one another.

There are no capital letters in Arabic.

Many letters in the Arabic language look alike. Sometimes the only difference between two letters is a dot above or below one of them. That dot is important. It changes the letter's sound. Most Arabic letters change shape slightly, depending on where they appear in a word.

# LETTERS OF THE ALPHABET
## *AND THEIR PRONUNCIATIONS*

أ • alif

ب بـ • baa'

ت تـ • taa'

ث ثـ • thaa'

ج جـ • jeem

ح حـ • haa'

خ خـ • khaa'

د • dal

ذ • zal

ر • raa'

ز • zay

س سـ • seen

ش شـ • sheen

ص صـ • saad

ض ضـ • daad

ط • taa'
(stronger than تـ ت)

ظ • zaa'

ع عـ • e'in

غ غـ • ghein

ف فـ • faa'

ق قـ • kwaff
(stronger than كـ ك)

ك كـ • kaff

ل لـ • lam

م مـ • meem

ن نـ • noon

ه هـ هـ ه • haa

و • waaw

ي يـ • yaa'

# IT SOUNDS LIKE

The Arabic alphabet has 28 letters. Many letters or sounds in Arabic do not exist in English. In their written form, Arabic letters sometimes include diacritics. These small marks above and below the letters stand for missing vowels. They help with pronunciation. The main diacritics are ◌َ ("fat-ha," a short a), ◌ِ ("kasra," a short i), ◌ُ ("damma," a short u), and ◌ّ ("shadda," the doubling of a sound, such as a double m or double r). In Arabic there are no silent letters.

| | SOUND | PRONUNCIATION | EXAMPLES | |
|---|---|---|---|---|
| **CONSONANTS** | ب / بـ | like b in banana | باب | bab |
| | ت / تـ | like t in tree | تاج | tag |
| | ث / ثـ | like th in earth | ثقيل | tha-QEEL |
| | ج / جـ | like j in Jack | جديد | ja-DEED |
| | ح / حـ | no match in English; the closest pronunciation is a strong h | فرح | FA-rah |
| | خ / خـ | no match in English; the closest pronunciation is kh in khan | خوخ | khokh |
| | د | like d in doctor | دولاب | do-LAB |
| | ذ | no match in English; the closest pronunciation is a strong z | لذيذ | la-ZEEZ |
| | ر | like r in ribbon | تراب | to-RAB |
| | ز | like z in amazed | جزر | JA-zar |
| | س / سـ | like s in seat | سور | soor |
| | ش / شـ | like sh in sheep | شجر | SHA-gar |
| | ص / صـ | no match in English; the closest pronunciation is a strong s | رصاص | ro-SAS |
| | ض / ضـ | no match in English; the closest pronunciation is a strong d | مضرب | MAD-rab |
| | ط | no match in English; the closest pronunciation is a strong t | مشط | mesht |
| | ظ | no match in English; the closest pronunciation is a strong z | ظرف | zarf |
| | ع / عـ | no match in English; the closest pronunciation is a strong a | عين | A'-in |
| | غ / غـ | no match in English; the closest pronunciation is g in yogurt | أغاني | a-GHA-ni |
| | ف / فـ | like f in fridge | فُرن | forn |
| | ق / قـ | no match in English; the closest pronunciation is a strong q | قطار | qe-TAR |
| | ك / كـ | like k in kite | كتاب | ke-TAB |
| | ل / لـ | like l in lazy | لبن | LA-ban |
| | م / مـ | like m in mum | مكتب | MAK-tab |
| | ن / نـ | like n in noon | بُنّي | BON-ni |
| | هـ / ه | like h in hair | هرم | HA-ram |
| **VOWELS** | ا | like a in cat | تفّاح | tof-FAH |
| | و | like u in prune | سكون | so-KOON |
| | ي / يـ | like ee in sheep | جميل | ja-MEEL |
| | ى | always appears at the end of a word; pronounced as a in hat | موسيقى | moo-SEE-qa |
| **VOWEL COMBINATIONS** | ◌َي | the ◌َ diacritic above a letter plus a ي at the end of a word is pronounced as ay in play | خَير | khayr |
| | ◌َو | the ◌َ diacritic above a letter plus a و is pronounced as aw in awesome | مَورد | MAW-red |

5

Hello.
مرحبًا.
(MAR-ha-ban)

Good morning.
صباح الخير.
(sa-BAH al-KHEIR)

Excuse me.
معذرةً.
(ma'-ZE-ra-tan)

Good night.
طابت ليلتك.
(TA-bat ly-LA-tok)

Good afternoon.
مساء الخير.
(ma-SAA' al-KHEIR)

Good-bye.
إلى اللقاء.
(I-la al-le-QAA')

Please.
من فضلك.
(men FAD-lek)

# Arabic: الأساسيات (al-ASA-se-yat)

Thank you.
شكرًا لك.
(SHU-kran lak)

You are welcome.
لا داعي للشكر.
(la DA'ie lel-shokr)

What is your name?
ما اسمك؟
(ma ES-mok)

My name is ___.
اسمي ____.
(ES-my ___)

**MORE TO LEARN**

| Yes | No |
|-----|-----|
| نعم | لا |
| (NA-a'm) | (la) |

Arabic: من أنت؟ (man AN-ta)

How old are you?
ما عمرك؟
(ma O'M-rak)

I am ___ years old.
لدى___أعوام.
(la-DAY ___ aa'-UAM)

I have a pet bird.
لدى عصفور.
(la-DAY o's-FOOR)

It does tricks.
إنه يقوم بحيل.
(e-NA-ho ya-QUM be-HE-yal)

dog
كلب
(KALB)

cat
قطة
(QET-ta)

11

Are you hungry?

هل تشعر بالجوع؟

(hal TASH-o'r bel-JOE')

I am hungry.

أنا جائع.

(A-na JA-e'e)

I am thirsty.

أنا عطشان.

(A-na A'T-shan)

What is for supper?

ما الذي سأتناوله في العشاء؟

(ma a-LA-zi sa'-a-ta-na-UA-la-ho fi al-a'-SHA')

lunch

الغداء

(al-gha-DAA')

breakfast

الإفطار

(al-EF-tar)

**MORE TO LEARN**

I am not hungry.

أنا لست جائعًا.

(A-na LAS-to ja-e-A'N)

12

# Arabic: الأُسرة (al-OS-ra)

Do you speak English?
هل تتحدث الإنجليزية؟
(hal ta-ta-HA-dath al-en-jli-ZE-ya)

French
الفرنسية
(al-fe-ren-SE-ya)

German
الألمانية
(al-al-ma-NE-ya)

Spanish
الإسبانية
(al-es-pa-NE-ya)

Chinese
الصينية
(assi-NE-ya)

DUTY FREE

A little.
قليلًا.
(qa-LI-lan)

## MORE TO LEARN

my father
أبي
(A-bi)

my sister
أختي
(OKH-ti)

my brother
أخي
(A-khi)

15

# Arabic: التاريخ والوقت (al-ta-RIKH wal-WAQT)

Today is Saturday.
اليوم هو السبت.
(al-yom HO-wa al-SABT)

Tomorrow is Sunday.
غدًا الأحد.
(gha-DAN al-a-HAD)

Yesterday was Friday.
أمس كان الجمعة.
(ams KA-na al-JOM-a'a)

**MORE TO LEARN**

Sunday
الأحد
(al-a-HAD)

Monday
الاثنين
(al-eth-NAYN)

Tuesday
الثلاثاء
(al-tho-la-THA')

Wednesday
الأربعاء
(al-ar-be-A'A)

Thursday
الخميس
(al-kha-MEES)

Friday
الجمعة
(al-JOM-a'a)

Saturday
السبت
(al-SABT)

17

**Arabic:** الشهور والفصول **(a-sho-HOOR wal-fo-SOOL)**

I love summer!
أنا أحب الصيف!
(A-na o-HEB al-SAYF)

fall
الخريف
(al-kha-REEF)

winter
الشتاء
(a-she-TAA')

spring
الربيع
(ar-ra-BIE')

**MORE TO LEARN**

January
يناير
(ya-NA-yer)

February
فبراير
(feb-RA-yer)

March
مارس
(MA-res)

April
أبريل
(AB-reel)

May
مايو
(MA-yo)

June
يونيو
(YON-yo)

July
يوليو
(YOL-yo)

August
أغسطس
(a-GHOS-tos)

September
سبتمبر
(seb-TEM-ber)

October
أكتوبر
(oc-TO-ber)

November
نوفمبر
(no-FEM-ber)

December
ديسمبر
(de-CEM-ber)

# Arabic: الطقس (al-TA-qs)

It is cold.
الجو بارد.
(al-JAW BA-red)

hot
حار
(har)

sunny
الشمس ساطعة
(a-SHAMS sa-TE-'ah)

Wear a coat.
ارتدِ المعطف.
(ER-ta-di al-ME'-taf)

boots
الحذاء الطويل
(al-he-ZAA' al-ta-WEEL)

a hat
القبعة
(al-ko-BA-a'h)

mittens
القفاز
(al-qo-FAZ)

21

We study science.

نحن نتعلم العلوم.

(NAH-noo na-ta-A'L-lam al-o'-LOOM)

math

الحساب

(al-he-SAB)

history

التاريخ

(al-ta-RIKH)

May I use your pencil?

أيمكنني استخدام قلمك الرصاص؟

(a-yom-KEN-ni es-tekh-DAM QA-la-mak al-ro-SAS)

scissors

مقصّك

(ma-QAS-sak)

glue

لصقك

(LAS-qak)

## MORE TO LEARN

My teacher is ___.

مدرستي هي ____.

(mo-da-RE-sa-ti HE-ya ___)

This is my favorite book!

هذا هو كتابي المفضل!

(HA-za HO-wa ke-TA-bi al-mo-FAD-dal)

Where are you?
أين أنت؟
(AY-na AN-ta)

I am in the kitchen.
أنا في المطبخ.
(A-na fel-MAT-bakh)

bathroom
الحمّام
(al-ham-MAM)

bedroom
غرفة النوم
(GHOR-fat al-NOOM)

living room
غرفة المعيشة
(GHOR-fat al-ma-A'l-sha)

dining room
غرفة الطعام
(GHOR-fat al-ta-A'M)

# Arabic: الهوايات (al-ho-wa-YAT)

What is your favorite book?
**ما هو كتابك المفضّل؟**
(ma HO-wa ke-TA-bak al-mo-FAD-dal)

TV show
**برنامج تليفزيوني**
(ber-NA-mej tli-fez-IO-ni)

Who is your favorite singer?
**من هو مطربك المفضّل؟**
(man HO-wa mot-RE-bak al-mo-FAD-dal)

What is your favorite movie?
**ما هو فيلمك المفضل؟**
(ma HO-wa FIL-mak al-mo-FAD-dal)

## MORE TO LEARN

Good luck!
**حظًا سعيدًا!**
(ha-ZAN sa-a'i-DAN)

Arabic: مع الأصدقاء (ma-A' al-as-de-QAA')

Let's go to the library.
هيا نذهب إلى المكتبة.
(HA-ya NAZ-hab I-la al-MAK-ta-ba)

store
المتجر
(ai-MAT-jar)

See you later!
أراك لاحقًا!
(a-RA-ka la-he-QAN)

Awesome!
مذهل!
(MOZ-hel)

# Numbers • الأعداد (al-A'-dad)

**1** one • واحد (WA-hid)

**2** two • اثنان (ith-NAN)

**3** three • ثلاثة (tha-LA-tha)

**4** four • أربعة (ar-BA-'a)

**5** five • خمسة (KHAM-sa)

**6** six • ستة (SIT-ta)

**7** seven • سبعة (SAB-a'a)

**8** eight • ثمانية (tha-MA-niya)

**9** nine • تسعة (TIS-a'h)

**10** ten • عشرة (A'-sha-ra)

**11** eleven • إحدى عشر (EH-da a'shr)

**12** twelve • اثنا عشر (eth-na A'-shar)

**13** thirteen • ثلاثة عشر (tha-la-that- A'-shar)

**14** fourteen • أربعة عشر (ar-ba-a'at- A'-shar)

**15** fifteen • خمسة عشر (kham-set A'-shar)

**16** sixteen • ستة عشر (set-tat-A'-shar)

**17** seventeen • سبعة عشر (sab-a'at A'-shar)

**18** eighteen • ثمانية عشر (tha-ma-ne-yat A'-shar)

**19** nineteen • تسعة عشر (tes-a'at A'-shar)

**20** twenty • عشرون (e'sh-ROON)

**30** thirty • ثلاثون (tha-la-THOON)

**40** forty • أربعون (ar-ba-'UN)

**50** fifty • خمسون (kham-SOON)

**60** sixty • ستون (se-TOON)

**70** seventy • سبعون (sab-U'N)

**80** eighty • ثمانون (tha-ma-NOON)

**90** ninety • تسعون (tes-O'ON)

**100** one hundred • مائة (MA-'a)

# COLORS • الألوان (al-AL-wan)

red • أحمر
(AH-mar)

purple • بنفسجي
(ba-NAF-se-jy)

orange • برتقالي
(bor-to-QA-ly)

pink • وردي
(WAR-di)

yellow • أصفر
(AS-far)

brown • بني
(BON-ni)

green • أخضر
(AKH-dar)

black • د
(AS-wad)

blue • أزرق
(AZ-raq)

white •
(AB-

# READ MORE

**Kudela, Katy R.** *My First Book of Arabic Words.* Bilingual Picture Dictionaries. Mankato, Minn.: Capstone Press, 2010.

**Melling, David.** *First Arabic Words.* Oxford; New York: Oxford University Press, 2009.

**Nunn, Daniel.** *Arabic.* Languages of the World. Chicago: Heinemann Library, 2012.

# INTERNET SITES

FactHound offers a safe, fun way to find Internet
...es related to this book. All of the sites on
...tHound have been researched by our staff.

... all you do:

...v.facthound.com

... is code: 9781404875173

 Check out projects, games and lots more at
**www.capstonekids.com**

## ALL THE BOOKS IN THE
## ...HER LANGUAGE! SERIES:

*...ST* ARABIC *PHRASES*

*...RST* FRENCH *PHRASES*

*...RST* GERMAN *PHRASES*

*...IRST* ITALIAN *PHRASES*

*...ST* JAPANESE *PHRASES*

Set Designer: Alison Thiele
Production Designer: Eric Manske
Art Director: Nathan Gassman
Production Specialist: Laura Manthe
The illustrations in this book were created digitally.

Picture Window Books
1710 Roe Crest Drive
North Mankato, Minnesota 56003
www.capstonepub.com

**Library of Congress Cataloging-in-Publication Data**
Kalz, Jill.
  My first Arabic phrases / by Jill Kalz ; illustrations by Daniele Fabbri.
    p. cm. — (Speak another language!)
  Text in both English and Arabic.
  ISBN 978-1-4048-7517-3 (library binding)
  ISBN 978-1-4048-7734-4 (paperback)
  ISBN 978-1-40487-995-9 (ebook PDF)
1. Arabic language—Textbooks for foreign speakers—English—Juvenile literature. 2. Arabic language—Conversation and phrase books—English—Juvenile literature.
I. Fabbri, Daniele, ill. II. Title.

  PJ6307.K29 2013
  492.7'82421—dc23                    2012008525

...the United States of America in North Mankato, Minnesota.
...GF12